Baldur

BY VIRGINIA LOH-HAGAN

Gods and goddesses were the main characters of myths. Myths are traditional stories from ancient cultures. Storytellers answered questions about the world by creating exciting explanations. People thought myths were true. Myths explained the unexplainable. They helped people make sense of human behavior and nature. Today, we use science to explain the world. But people still love myths. Myths may not be literally true. But they have meaning. They tell us something about our history and culture.

Published in the United States of America by Cherry Lake Publishing
Ann Arbor, Michigan
www.cherrylakepublishing.com

Content Adviser: Alexandra Krasowski, Worcester Art Museum, Harvard University (Extension School)
Reading Adviser: Marla Conn MS, Ed., Literacy specialist, Read-Ability, Inc.
Book Design: Jen Wahi

Photo Credits: © vlastas/Shutterstock.com, 5; © Vuk Kostic/Shutterstock.com, 6, 7, 29; Carl Emil Doepler/Public Domain/Wikimedia Commons, 8; © Nejron Photo/Shutterstock.com, 11; Johannes Flintoe/Public Domain/Wikimedia Commons, 13; © Nejron Photo/Shutterstock.com, 19; © patrimonio designs ltd/Shutterstock.com, 21; © Algol/Shutterstock.com, 23; © Zacarias Pereira da Mata/Shutterstock.com, 24; © W.G. Collingwood/Public Domain/Wikimedia Commons, 27; © Howard David Johnson, 2018, Cover, 1, 15; Various art elements throughout, Shutterstock.com

Copyright © 2019 by Cherry Lake Publishing
All rights reserved. No part of this book may be reproduced or utilized in any form or by any means without written permission from the publisher.

45th Parallel Press is an imprint of Cherry Lake Publishing.

Library of Congress Cataloging-in-Publication Data

Names: Loh-Hagan, Virginia, author.
Title: Baldur / by Virginia Loh-Hagan.
Description: Ann Arbor : Cherry Lake Publishing, 2018. | Series: Gods and goddesses of the ancient world | Includes bibliographical references and index.
Identifiers: LCCN 2018003333 | ISBN 9781534129436 (hardcover) | ISBN 9781534131132 (pdf) | ISBN 9781534132634 (pbk.) | ISBN 9781534134331 (hosted ebook)
Subjects: LCSH: Balder (Norse deity)—Juvenile literature.
Classification: LCC BL870.B3 L64 2018 | DDC 293/.2113—dc23
LC record available at https://lccn.loc.gov/2018003333

Printed in the United States of America
Corporate Graphics

ABOUT THE AUTHOR:

Dr. Virginia Loh-Hagan is an author, university professor, former classroom teacher, and curriculum designer. She's obsessed with twins. She lives in San Diego with her very tall husband and very naughty dogs. To learn more about her, visit www.virginialoh.com.

TABLE OF CONTENTS

ABOUT THE AUTHOR 2

CHAPTER 1:
ROYAL ROOTS 4

CHAPTER 2:
MURDER, HE WROTE! 10

CHAPTER 3:
TO HELL AND BACK 16

CHAPTER 4:
NO PLACE LIKE HOME 22

CHAPTER 5:
THE END OF THE WORLD 26

DID YOU KNOW? 30
CONSIDER THIS! 31
LEARN MORE 31
GLOSSARY 32
INDEX 32

CHAPTER 1

ROYAL ROOTS

Who is Baldur? Who is his family?

Baldur was a **Norse** god. Norse means from the Norway area. Baldur was the god of peace. He was the god of light. He was the god of the summer sun. He gave off light. He was pure. He was good. He was handsome. He was kind. He was generous. He was cheerful. He was loved by all the gods. He was loved by all humans. He could do no wrong.

Baldur was part of the most important Norse god family. His father was Odin. Odin was a powerful god. He was a creator god. He created the world. He was the father of all gods. He was the father of all humans. He was called "All father."

Baldur's mother was Frigg. Frigg was the goddess of marriage. She was Odin's wife. She helped him rule.

Vikings lived in Norway. They worshiped gods like Baldur.

Baldur came from a big family.

Baldur had a **twin** brother. Twins are people born at the same time. Baldur's twin was named Hod. Hod was blind. He lived in darkness. He was the god of darkness. He was the god of night. He was the opposite of Baldur. Baldur was the light in the darkness. His smile brought light to everyone. Light shone wherever he went.

Odin had children with many women. This means Baldur had many half brothers. Thor was Baldur's half brother.

Family Tree

Grandparents: Borr (god of mountains) and Bestla (goddess of water and ice)

Parents: Odin (father of gods) and Frigg (goddess of marriage)

Brothers: Hod (god of winter and darkness, often called Hodr), Hermod (messenger of the gods), and Thor (half brother, god of thunder)

Spouse: Nanna (goddess of joy and peace)

Child: Forseti (god of justice, peace, and truth)

Thor was the god of thunder. He was Baldur's most famous family member.

Baldur married Nanna. Nanna was beautiful. She was the goddess of joy. She was the goddess of peace. In some stories, Baldur and Hod both wanted Nanna. They fought over her. Baldur won.

Baldur and Nanna had a son. His name was Forseti. Forseti means "chairman." Forseti was the god of justice. He was the god of peace. He was the god of truth. He was wise. He spoke well. He helped people solve fights. He sat in his **hall**. Halls are like grand houses. He gave fair judgments. People lived in safety if they followed his orders.

 Like Baldur, Forseti was a gentle god.

CHAPTER 2
MURDER, HE WROTE!

How did Frigg help Baldur? How did Baldur die?

Everyone loved Baldur. He was everyone's favorite. He was Frigg's favorite son.

Baldur had dreams of dying. He dreamed of doom. He saw his own death. He told his parents. Frigg was worried. She made a list of everything that could harm Baldur. She went all around the world. She begged people not to hurt Baldur. She got them to promise to keep him safe. Baldur was well-liked. People listened. They agreed.

But Frigg didn't think mistletoe was a problem. She thought mistletoe wasn't important. She thought it was too little to do any harm.

Frigg went back to the gods' meeting hall. She told Baldur he was safe. She hosted a party. The gods were happy. They were in a good mood. They wanted to test Baldur's protection. A god threw a rock at Baldur. The rock bounced off. Baldur didn't get hurt. The gods thought this was fun. They turned it into a game. They threw all kinds of things at Baldur. They even threw weapons at him.

Hod might have been a little jealous of his brother.

All in the Family

Brunhilde was a Valkyrie. Valkyries were dark angels of death. They flew over battlefields. They took the strong warriors. They took them to the underworld. They worked for Odin. Brunhilde was strong and beautiful. She was supposed to work for Odin. But she rejected him. She didn't listen. Odin punished her. He made her fall into a deep sleep. He surrounded her with a wall of fire. Sigurd was a Norse hero. He crossed the fire wall. He kissed Brunhilde. This woke her up. They got married. Sigurd traveled. He drank a magic potion. He forgot about Brunhilde. He married someone else. His new wife's brother wanted to marry Brunhilde. He asked for Sigurd's help. Brunhilde didn't like being tricked. She had Sigurd killed. Then she missed him. She threw herself into Sigurd's funeral fire. This was so she could join him in death.

The gods liked to play games. They got bored easily.

Everything bounced off him. Nothing hurt him.

Loki was another god. He liked playing tricks. He tricked Frigg. Frigg told him about mistletoe. Loki used that information. He made a mistletoe dart.

Loki saw Hod sitting by himself. He gave Hod the dart. He helped guide Hod's hand. Hod threw the mistletoe dart at Baldur. He didn't think it would hurt Baldur. But the dart pierced him. Baldur fell down. He died.

Loki ran away. Everyone was sad. They cried. They blamed Hod. Baldur's light was gone. This created winter.

Odin was mad. He wanted to get even. He had a son with a **giantess**. A giantess is a female giant. The son's name was Vali. Vali grew up in one day. His job was to kill Hod. He shot Hod with an arrow.

 Vikings mainly traveled by ships.

CHAPTER 3

TO HELL AND BACK

How was Baldur's death mourned? What was the deal Hel made with Hermod?

Everyone **mourned** Baldur's death. To mourn is to show deep sadness. A **funeral** fire was created. Funerals are events that happen when someone dies. They honor someone's life. Funeral fires turn dead bodies into ashes.

Nanna was sad. She missed Baldur. She threw herself into the fire. She wanted to be with Baldur. Baldur's horse also jumped in the fire.

All this happened on Baldur's ship. Baldur's things were added to his ship. People also added gifts. The ship became very heavy.

The ship wouldn't move. It was stuck. So, a giantess helped. The giantess was named Hyrrokkin. She rode in on a wolf.

Giants were another tribe of gods.

She pushed the ship. Fire came off the ship. This shook the earth.

Hermod was one of Baldur's brothers. He was the messenger of the gods. Odin and Frigg gave Hermod a job. They told him to go to the **underworld**. The underworld is where dead souls live. It's also called hell. It was ruled by Hel. Hel was the daughter of Loki and a giantess.

Hermod rode Odin's horse. He rode for 9 days. He went to hell. He entered the gates of death. He saw Baldur. Baldur was sitting next to Hel. He kneeled before Hel. He begged for Baldur's life. He said Baldur was beloved and missed. Hel wanted him to prove it. She made a deal. She would release Baldur if all living things cried for him.

 Sometimes, gods and goddesses asked for help.

Real World Connection

Baldur and Hod were twins. They were special. They were gods. But they were not the only special twins. Mike and Jim Lanier are twins. They're identical. They have a world record. They're the world's tallest twins. They're 7 feet and 7 inches (2.3 meters) tall. They wear size 17 shoes. They each weigh about 360 pounds (163 kilograms). They played basketball. They have acromegaly. This means they'll never stop growing. They won't grow taller. But their body parts may grow bigger. There's another set of special twins. Claire and Ann Recht are the world's tallest female twins. They're 6 feet and 7 inches (2 m) tall. They play volleyball. They can jump 10 feet (3 m). Their parents are over 6 feet (1.8 m) tall. Their house has extra-tall showers. It's not easy being tall.

Odin's horse had eight legs.

Frigg and the other gods begged everyone to cry for Baldur. But Loki stepped in. He disguised himself as Thok. Thok was a giantess. She refused to cry. So, Baldur couldn't return to the land of the living. He and his wife stayed in the underworld.

CHAPTER 4
NO PLACE LIKE HOME

What was Hringhorn? What was Breidablik? What was Glitnir?

Baldur had a special ship. It was named Hringhorn. This means "ring-horn." The ship's **prow** had rings of horns. A prow is the front of a ship. The ship's **mast** had iron rings. Masts are long poles. These poles support the sails.

Hringhorn was the greatest ship ever built. It was the world's largest ship.

Baldur was a sun god. Hringhorn looked like a sun's circle. Baldur's funeral fire looked like a sunset. Baldur sailed on Hringhorn into his death. His last trip represented a journey to the dead.

Baldur lived in **Asgard**. Asgard was the universe's center. It was where Aesir gods lived. There were two tribes of Norse gods and goddesses. They were the Aesir and the Vanir. The Vanir lived in Vanaheim.

Baldur could live on his ship.

Baldur lived in a beautiful house.
He owned beautiful things.

Baldur and Nanna lived in Breidablik. This means "gleaming." This was the name of their hall. Breidablik was the most beautiful hall. Everything in it was beautiful. Nothing impure could live in it. Impure means dirty or bad. Nobody could tell a lie in the hall. Nobody could do anything unkind.

Baldur's son also had a hall. It was called Glitnir. This means "shining." The hall had silver ceilings. It had golden pillars. It shined out light. The light could be seen from far away.

Cross-Cultural Connection

Osiris was an ancient Egyptian god. He ruled Egypt. His brother was Seth. Seth was also a god. He was jealous of Osiris. He wanted to rule Egypt. He killed Osiris. He ripped him into pieces. He flung them all over Egypt. Osiris's wife and sister found all the pieces. They buried most of the body parts. But they kept some parts. They used these parts to bring him back to life. Osiris became king of the underworld. He ruled the dead. He had the power to grant life from the underworld. He made plants grow. He caused the flooding of the Nile River. He renewed life. Osiris's son tried to get even. He fought Seth. Then he ruled Egypt.

CHAPTER 5
THE END OF THE WORLD

What was Ragnarok? What does Baldur's death mean?

There aren't many stories about Baldur. He is most famous for his death.

Odin could see the future. He knew Baldur would die. But he couldn't protect his son. He couldn't stop his death from happening.

Baldur's death was the loss of light and truth. It was the end of the world. It was a warning sign for **Ragnarok**. This was the final war. It was also known as the "doom of the gods." The gods weren't **immortal**. Immortal means living forever.

Gods fought. They died. They destroyed the world. There were earthquakes. There were fires. There were floods. Water covered the world. Then the world would start again.

During Ragnarok, the gates between the living and the dead were weak. So, Baldur left the underworld. He fought in the last battle. He survived the war. After Ragnarok, Baldur was reborn. This was the beginning of a new age.

Baldur's death was the beginning of the end for the gods.

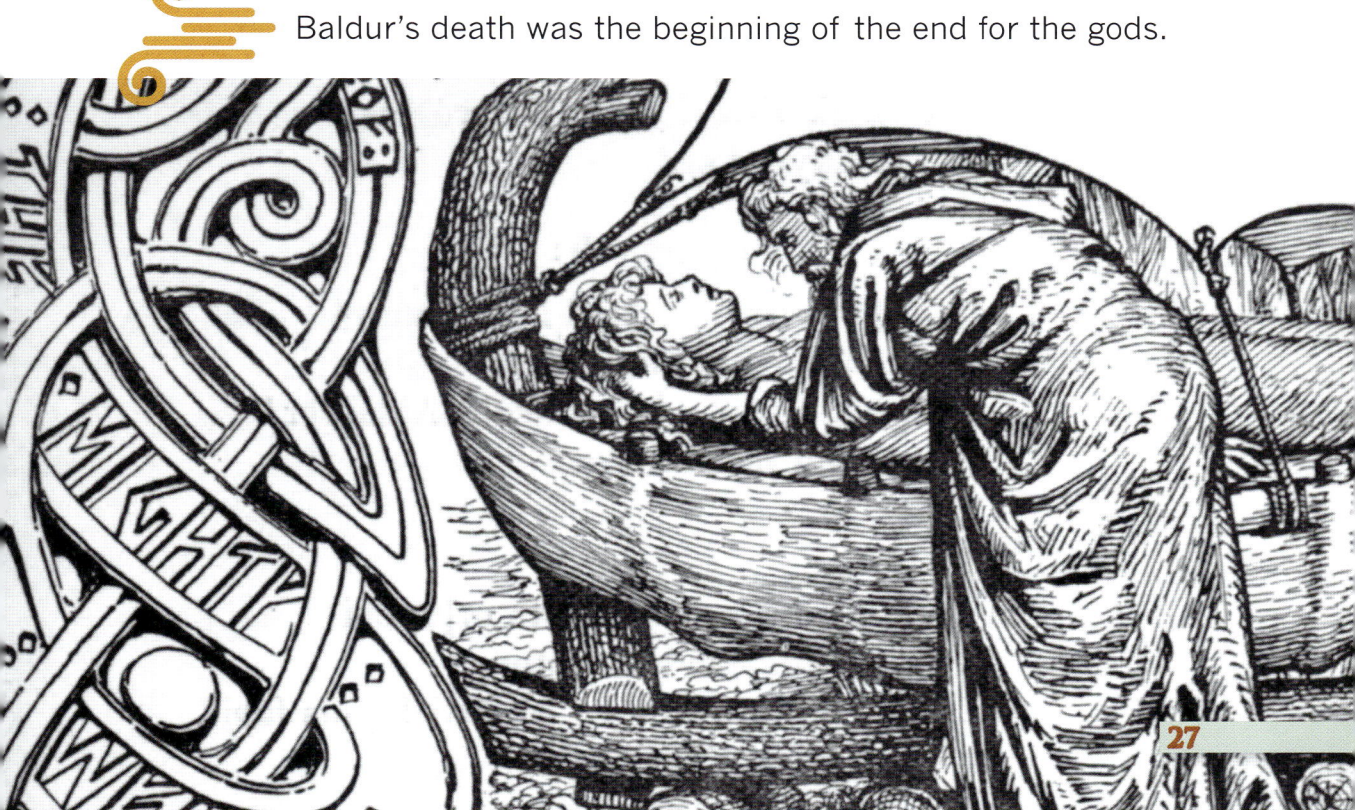

Some people think the gods planned Baldur's death. Loki had Baldur killed to save him. Baldur was kept safe in the

Explained By Science

Mistletoe is often hung at Christmas time. People kiss under it. But it's not safe. Mistletoe berries have poison. They shouldn't be eaten. They shouldn't be made into a tea. They slow down the heart rate. They blur vision. They cause stomach pain. They cause diarrhea. They cause hallucinations. Hallucinations are when people see things that aren't there. Mistletoe can also be deadly. It's most harmful for children and pets. There have been over 1,700 mistletoe poisoning cases in the United States. If used correctly, mistletoe can be used as medicine. Mistletoe is also a parasite. Parasites live off other living things. They suck the life out of something else. Mistletoe has small green leaves. They grow directly from the tree trunk. Their seeds send roots into the tree. They feed off the tree. They take the tree's water. Sometimes this can hurt the tree.

Ragnarok was a cycle of destruction and creation.

underworld until the war. The gods needed Baldur to help rule in the new world. The gods knew what they were doing.

Don't anger the gods. Baldur had great powers. And he knew how to use them.

DID YOU KNOW?

- Baldur has been called Baldur the Brave.
- There's a different version to Baldur's story. Baldur and Hod were human princes. They fought over a princess named Nanna. They had a duel. Hod had a sword named Mistletoe. He killed Baldur. He married Nanna.
- Baldur was also the god of forgiveness.
- People worshiped Baldur. They would light a candle in the dark. They called his name.
- Baldur wanted people to be kind. It's especially important to be kind to people who are unkind.
- There were two tribes of Norse gods and goddesses. They were the Vanir and the Aesir. Baldur was the most beautiful of the Aesir gods. The Aesir and Vanir didn't trust each other. They went to war. The Aesir fought with weapons and force. The Vanir fought with magic. The war lasted for years. They got tired of fighting. They made a peace deal. They traded prisoners.
- Baldur also had healing powers. He knew how to use herbs.
- Thor was at Baldur's funeral. He was really upset. He lost control. He kicked a dwarf into the funeral fire.

CONSIDER THIS!

TAKE A POSITION! Think about how Baldur died. How guilty was Hod? Do you blame Hod? Why or why not? Argue your point with reasons and evidence.

SAY WHAT? Baldur and Hod were twin brothers. Learn more about Hod. Compare them. Explain how they're the same. Explain how they're different.

THINK ABOUT IT! Baldur was an important god. But there aren't as many myths about him. Write your own myth about Baldur.

LEARN MORE

Bowen, Carl, Michael Dahl, and Louise Simonson. *Gods and Thunder: A Graphic Novel of Old Norse Myths.* North Mankato, MN: Capstone Young Readers, 2017.

Napoli, Donna Jo, and Christina Balit (illus.). *Treasury of Norse Mythology: Stories of Intrigue, Trickery, Love, and Revenge.* Washington, DC: National Geographic, 2015.

GLOSSARY

Asgard (AHS-gahrd) center of the universe where the Aesir gods lived

funeral (FYOO-ner-uhl) a ceremony held after someone dies that honors that person's life

giantess (JYE-uhn-tis) female giant

hall (HAWL) grand house

immortal (ih-MOR-tuhl) living forever

impure (im-PYOOR) unclean, dirty, evil

mast (MAHST) a long pole that supports a ship's sails

mourned (MORND) to show deep sadness

Norse (NORS) coming from the Norway area

prow (PROU) front of a ship

Ragnarok (RAHG-nuh-rok) the final battle of the gods' world, marking the end of their world

twin (TWIN) person born at the same time as another person from the same mother

underworld (UHN-der-wurld) the place where dead souls live

INDEX

A
Asgard, 23

B
Baldur, 30
    death of, 14–17, 22, 26, 27–29
    family, 4–9
    how Frigg helped him, 10–11
    rebirth of, 27–29
    in the underworld, 18–21
    where he lived after death, 23–25
    who he is, 4–9
Breidablik, 23–25

F
Forseti, 7, 9
Frigg, 5, 7, 10–11, 13, 18, 21

H
Hel, 18
Hermod, 7, 18
Hod, 6, 7, 9, 11, 14, 20, 30

L
Loki, 13–14, 18, 21, 28

M
mistletoe, 10, 13–14, 28

N
Nanna, 7, 9, 16, 23, 30

O
Odin, 4–5, 7, 12, 14, 18, 26

R
Ragnarok, 26–27

T
Thor, 7, 9, 30

U
underworld, 12, 18, 21, 27, 29